Rock'n PopStars

Paul
McCartney

by M. HOWARD GELFAND

❤ Creative Education

Published by Creative Education, 123 South Broad Street, Mankato, Minnesota 56001.

Library of Congress Number: 83-71564   ISBN: 0-89813-100-6

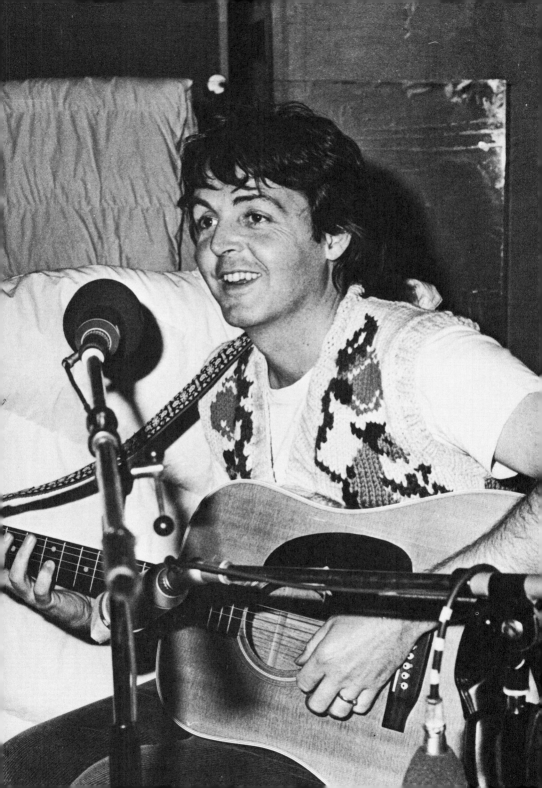

There was a boy growing up in England not too long ago. He was an ordinary boy who did well in school and liked music.

The boy's father had been a musician himself once, and he was pleased that his son wanted to play. The father, a cotton salesman, didn't have much money, but he saved enough to buy a trumpet for his son.

At first the boy was enthusiastic about learning to play this new instrument. Then he discovered that the trumpet made his upper lip sore. A sore upper lip made it hard to sing, which the boy loved to do. So that ended his career as a trumpet player.

The father was disappointed. After his wife's death the year before, he had only the boy and his younger brother to give him a reason to keep on going. He had high hopes for his sons.

But the father didn't lose hopes when the boy, now 15, traded his trumpet for a guitar. Others regarded the guitar as an inferior instrument—one played by a new breed called "Teddy Boys." Many people said that Teddy Boys wore their hair too long and their pants too tight.

The father, however, loved all sorts of music, and he was as eager to teach as the boy was to learn. The boy did poorly, at first, but he soon figured out what was wrong. Although right-handed, he could strum the guitar only with his left hand. In no time he was playing the guitar whenever he could, even in the bathtub. Late at night, with his father and brother both asleep, he softly strummed its strings.

The boy joined a band and started writing his own rock and roll songs. Pretty soon the band was playing at dances and getting paid for it. From then on, the boy decided, his name would be "Paul Ramon." The band was called "Johnny and the Moondogs."

After a while the boy went back to using his real name, Paul McCartney. And the band changed its name to the Beatles. The rest, as they say, is history.

Today Paul McCartney is the only one of the four Beatles still working full-time on music. Paul's

band, Wings, is very popular these days. In fact, there are now people who don't even realize that McCartney made music history long before Wings.

It is unlikely, though, that Wings will ever be as popular as the Beatles. In fact, there may never be a group as popular as the Beatles. Paul himself is listed in the Guinness Book of World Records as the most successful composer and recording artist of all time.

John Paul McCartney was born on June 18, 1942, in northwest England in the town of Liverpool. His mother, Mary, returned to her work as a maternity nurse soon after Paul was born. The McCartneys saved enough money to buy a small house. Paul eventually did so well in school that Jim McCartney decided his older son should go to college someday — something few of Paul's friends would do.

Jim McCartney's hopes for Paul might have been realized if Paul hadn't gone to a church hall one day. He went to see a band called the Quarry Men. One member, a boy named John Lennon, was a fine singer but he never seemed to know all the words to the songs. After the show, Paul went backstage and wrote out the words to some songs and gave them to John.

Pretty soon Paul was a member of the Quarry Men. But he was not an instant success. In his first appearance with the group, he made a lot of mistakes during his important guitar solo. So he was switched from lead guitar to rhythm guitar.

Paul was now spending more time playing the guitar and less time studying his school books. Still, he continued to do well in school until he was 17, when George Harrison joined the group and they started to call themselves the Rainbows. When they got tired of that name they switched to "Johnny and the Moondogs."

That wasn't quite right either, so when they got their first professional offer, they were looking for another name. They wanted this name to be right, because they were about to play in Scotland for two weeks. The name they chose would stick. When they settled on the Beatles, their friends said they should find a longer name. They switched to

the Silver Beatles, but finally went back to simply the Beatles.

The Scotland trip didn't make stars out of the Beatles, but it did make them into musicians. College was out of the question now. The Beatles were getting lots of offers, even though none paid much.

Soon they were off to Germany, where the Beatles played in an old, run-down night club. This was not exactly the big time. They had to sleep in an old movie theater, in tiny rooms right next to a toilet. It was so cold that they slept in their leather jackets. Fortunately, the engagement didn't last long. They soon got an offer to play in another club and quickly accepted.

As they moved out of the theater, the Beatles' drummer, Pete Best, accidentally burned a hole in some old drapes. A short time later, the police arrested Paul and Pete for setting the fire. The fire had caused little damage, but the club's owner wanted to get back at the Beatles for going to work for someone else. Paul and Pete weren't charged with anything, but the police drove them to the airport and made them return to England.

When Paul returned home it was near Christmas of 1960. He was 18 now—old enough for a regular job. His father encouraged Paul to get work loading packages onto delivery trucks—the first "real" job he ever had.

And the last. Two weeks later George and John had also returned home, and the Beatles were back together. Playing before loud and sometimes drunken crowds in Germany had changed them all. Now they played with more energy and more confidence. Paul and John both started writing, and some of their songs were pretty good. "Love Me Do," and "PS I Love You" are samples.

Pete Best was replaced by Ringo Starr, and the Beatles started to attract fans. When they appeared on a British TV show in early 1962, the audience— especially the girls—loved them. Unlike other musicians who looked seriously into the camera, the Beatles laughed, making funny faces, bouncing around, shaking their long hair.

Later that year, the Beatles cut their first single: "Love Me Do," with "PS I Love You" on the flip side. The record was a mild success in England, reaching Number 17 on the charts.

At the time, the Beatles weren't getting much attention in the U.S. This was true even after they had their first Number One single in Britain. American record companies were unimpressed with "Please Please Me." One record company executive responded to the song by noting, "We don't think the Beatles will do anything in this market" (meaning America).

Only one year later, the Beatles were the most popular band in the entire world. In fact, their music traveled from England to America like a tidal wave. In 1964 "I Wanna Hold Your Hand" was their first record released in the U.S. By the time the year was over, "I Wanna Hold Your Hand" had sold a million copies. And in that year the Beatles accomplished the incredible feat of having six Number One hits in the U.S.

The Beatles were now ready to make their first trip to America—and America was certainly ready

for them. The reception they got was unlike anything the U.S. had ever seen before. Arriving in New York, they found more than 10,000 screaming fans gathered at the airport.

Wherever they played the screams continued. Most of the time, it was impossible to hear what the Beatles were singing. But that didn't seem to matter. The crowds just wanted a look.

The Beatles became more than a rock and roll band. Other groups started copying their style. Schoolboys dressed like them. School teachers and principals complained when boys started wearing "Beatle haircuts." They considered long hair indecent. Students all across America were told to cut their hair or at least comb it out of their eyes.

Yet when you look at pictures of the Beatles in those days, it's hard to see what everyone was so upset about. The Beatles in those days had hair that looks short today.

The reason that "Beatle haircuts" are acceptable today is that the Beatles made them acceptable. Many of those teachers who were so upset in

1964, have hair today that isn't much shorter than the Beatles' hair was then.

Up until 1964, the Beatles were all more or less equal. John had been the unofficial leader since the beginning, but Paul, Ringo, and George were equally popular. As the Beatles became more famous, Paul started to emerge as a leader. Paul was the best at talking with reporters. Along with John, he was the songwriter and singer. This was especially important because by now the Beatles were no longer performing many songs written by others. Also, Paul was usually considered to be the best looking of the four.

Looking back, it seems that the friendship between Paul and John began coming apart in the mid-1960's. This was a time when everything the Beatles did became an instant success. John was more serious than Paul. While John's songs were about politicians or drugs, Paul's were more likely love songs.

But Paul was experimenting, too. He took up the piano, though he continued to play the guitar and sometimes the drums. And in 1965 Paul wrote a song that was accompanied by a string quartet. This most unusual rock and roll song was "Yesterday," and by now it has been recorded by nearly 2,000 other performers.

By now the Beatles had everything they ever wanted. Especially Paul—who had said more than once that all he wanted out of life was a few hundred dollars, just enough for an old car, a guitar, and a place to live.

Despite their almost unbelievable success, the Beatles were not happy. Yet it seemed they could go on making Number One songs forever.

Perhaps this was the problem. They wanted to do something else. Like many people who get what they always wanted, they found out that it couldn't make them happy. As the 1960's moved into the 1970's, John and George were bored with their success and their fans. Not Paul, however, He still loved to perform and he still loved the fans. Sometimes, when teenage girls gathered in front of his house hoping to get a look at him, he opened a window and sang "Yesterday" for them.

The Beatles were no longer performing in public, which frustrated Paul. He thought they owed it to their fans to do concerts. Paul missed performing so much that one day he shocked the customers of a local pub by giving a brief concert on the pub's piano.

Around this time Paul realized that he was the only one trying to keep the Beatles together. It was a job that couldn't last long. Fortunately, something happened to ease his dissappointment: he met a photographer named Linda Eastman.

A year older than Paul, Linda was not among the women who screamed for the Beatles or camped out on Paul's lawn. Married when she was

18, she was divorced and had a daughter named Heather.

As Linda and Paul got to know one another, Paul grew very fond of Heather. He loved to read her stories and to play his guitar for her. Family life was right for Paul. In March of 1969 he married Linda. In the years to come they would have three other children, two girls and a boy.

As Paul settled into married life, he was still trying desperately to keep the Beatles together. He knew they would probably never play another concert, but he hoped they could still record. By themselves, each of the Beatles was a fine musician. Together, though, they were great. Although they did not get along so well anymore, they managed another album in 1970, *Abbey Road*. They argued a lot, though, when they recorded the album. It was clear that John, especially, was no longer interested in being a Beatle.

Paul was depressed. He wasn't sure what he'd do without the Beatles. Finally Linda convinced him that he should start working on records of his own. John made it clear that he was through being a Beatle, and Ringo and George were also bored. Paul really didn't have much choice.

On April 9, 1970, the most popular band in the world was a band no more. Paul phoned John, telling him he was quitting. Then Paul sent a statement to the London newspapers. PAUL QUITS BEATLES, the newspapers announced the next day. And suddenly everyone was mad at Paul.

John was angry because he had already decided to quit. He thought Paul was just trying to get attention. Beatle fans were upset because they blamed Paul for the end of the Beatles. And Paul didn't expect to please the critics, because everything he did after that would be compared to what the Beatles had done.

Sure enough, Paul's first album, *McCartney*, was criticized by reviewers. John Lennon told one reporter that Paul now sounded like Engelbert Humperdinck. And John was a Humperdinck fan.

Still, Paul's first album became a Number One seller. A year later Paul released another album,

Ram. This was not as popular with the fans, but it was just as unpopular with the critics. To make things worse, John came out with an album of his own a few months later. *Imagine* contained one song that was an attack on Paul. In the song, John sings: "A pretty face may last a year or two, but pretty soon they'll see what you can do."

Paul's career was going nowhere, and he knew it. Some musicians might have blamed the critics, but Paul realized that he needed to form a band and test his music by performing live. This was how the Beatles had done it.

But Paul went ahead with a third album, *Wild Life.* This was even less successful than *Ram.* Paul's career hit rock bottom.

Instead of quitting Paul took his new group, Wings, on a trip across England. It was one of the more unusual trips that a rock and roll group has taken. Wings traveled on a bus, stopping to perform whenever they felt like it.

Just as the tour of Germany had improved the Beatles, this tour seemed to help Wings. Their first album, *Red Rose Speedway,* became Number One even though the critics didn't care for it. They were especially critical of Linda, who sings harmony on the album.

Wings was becoming quite popular in both England and America. Number One hits came one after another: "My Love," "Band on the Run," "Listen to What the Man Said," "Silly Love Songs."

At last, the fans and the critics were accepting Paul as himself, not as an ex-Beatle. Not that people had forgotten about the Beatles. John, Paul, George, and Ringo were still offered up to $50 million to do a concert together.

Paul knew that many people came to his concerts just because he used to be a Beatle. But as he once said, "It doesn't matter why they came, it's what they think when they go home." If Paul had any doubts about what they thought, he must have felt better when *Red Rose Speedway* became the top-selling album in the U.S. In fact, *Red Rose Speedway* replaced a collection of old Beatles' songs as Number One.

READERS' AWARD
FOR THE OUTSTANDING MUSIC PERSONALITY

By 1974 even the critics were starting to love Paul and Wings. His new album, *Band on the Run*, was a top seller in just about every country. One important critic wrote that *Band on the Run* was "the finest record yet released by any of the four musicians who were once called the Beatles."

Paul enjoyed the praise, though he was disappointed to be compared to the Beatles once again. To prove himself and his band, Paul decided to make a tour of the U.S. Paul had last been on an American stage in 1966, when the Beatles made their final U.S. tour. Now, 10 years later, Paul McCartney and Wings were back again.

The tour was a success even before the Wings left England, the concerts all sold out. Everywhere Wings went, crowds cheered. It made no difference whether they were playing new songs or old Beatles numbers.

This was a time when many rock and roll bands — especially punk bands — were getting attention with wild onstage antics like setting fire to their guitars or insulting their audiences. Wings proved that they didn't need that sort of thing. Paul also showed how much he respected his fans by spending hours before each concert making sure everything was just right. His hard work paid off. One critic wrote, "Paul McCartney has proved that he could make it on his own."

A the age of 33, Paul was no longer an ex-Beatle. He was, once more, just Paul McCartney.

Paul's life hasn't changed much since that first Wings' tour of the U.S. He has more money and more gray hair now, but he doesn't seem to care about either. When he isn't performing or recording, he's likely to be playing "How Much Is That Doggy in the Window" for his kids. Expensive paintings hang on his walls, with finger paintings by the children next to them. He likes to sit around the house in blue jeans and a sweater, reading science fiction or watching T.V.

Paul has two houses now, one in England and the other in Scotland. The house in Scotland is up on a hill, far from the main road. Ducks and geese roam around, and there are sheep that Paul some-times shears himself.

In 1978 Paul wrote a song expressing his love for his home in Scotland. Called "Mull of Kintyre," it became the biggest-selling record in British history. Before "Mull of Kintyre," the most successful in British song had been "She Loves You"—by the Beatles, of course.

Today people might still be hoping that they would get together again, except that on December 8, 1980, John Lennon was killed by a crazy man with a gun.

The reunion can never happen now. But the Beatles' music will live forever on their records. And Paul's own music is still very much alive.

Paul is still criticized by people who think his records aren't serious enough. In one of his most popular songs, Paul answers these critics:

> *You'd think that people would have had enough of silly love songs,*
> *But I look around me and I see it isn't so;*
> *Some people want to fill the world with silly love songs.*
> *And what's wrong with that*
> *I'd like to know.*